T0109764

What is That Noise?

Practicing the OI Sound

Isabella Garcia

Rosen
PHONICS
READERS

Rosen
Classroom™

Roy is sleeping in his bed.
Then he hears a noise.

Now Roy is awake.
What is that noise?

Is it a cowboy outside?
What noise do cowboys make?

Roy does not think
it is a cowboy.

Some of Roy's toys make noise.
Is it a toy?

Roy's toys do not make
that noise.

Joy is Roy's sister.
Is Joy making noise?

Joy is sleeping.

Joy is not making noise.

Roy listens to the noise again.
It is a voice.

Roy joins his mom and dad.
"You are noisy!" he says.

Now Roy can enjoy his sleep.